D0609387

AUG 1 5 2003

THE ATTACK ON U.S. SERVICEMEN IN SAUDI ARABIA ON JUNE 25, 1996

Amanda Ferguson

The Rosen Publishing Group, Inc.
New York

THIS BOOK IS THE PROPERTY OF
THE NATIONAL CITY PUBLIC LIBRARY

For Kevin

Published in 2003 by The Rosen Publishing Group, Inc.
29 East 21st Street, New York, NY 10010

Copyright © 2003 by The Rosen Publishing Group, Inc.

First Edition

All rights reserved. No part of this book may be reproduced in any form without permission in writing from the publisher, except by a reviewer.

Library of Congress Cataloging-in-Publication Data

Ferguson, Amanda.
The attack on U.S. servicemen in Saudi Arabia on June 25, 1996/by Amanda Ferguson—1st ed.
    p. cm.—(Terrorist attacks)
Includes bibliographical references and index.
Contents: Saudi Arabia: a land of tradition in changing times—Relations between the United States and Saudi Arabia—The Riyadh bombing—Khobar Towers—Investigation into the Khobar Towers bombing—Global terrorism: a new era in foreign relations.
ISBN 0-8239-3861-1 (library binding)
1. Dhahran Military Housing Facility Bombing, Dhahran, Saudi Arabia, 1996. 2. Terrorism—Saudi Arabia. 3. Bombing investigation—Saudi Arabia. [1. Dhahran Military Housing Facility Bombing, Dhahran, Saudi Arabia, 1996. 2. Terrorism—Saudi Arabia. 3. Saudi Arabia—Relations—United States. 4. United States—Relations—Saudi Arabia.]
I. Title. II. Series.
HV6433.S33F47 2003
953.8—dc21

                                                  2002011662

Manufactured in the United States of America

CONTENTS

INTRODUCTION

At 10:30 PM on June 25, 1996, soldiers and civilians housed at Saudi Arabia's King Abdul-Aziz Naval Air Base in Al-Khobar in Saudi Arabia's eastern province were getting ready to turn in for the night. Most didn't notice the two suspicious vehicles that drove up to the Khobar housing complex. But Sergeant Alfredo Guerreo, a twenty-nine-year-old U.S. Air Force serviceman standing guard that night, did. Perched on the roof, Guerreo watched a tanker truck and a car drive up slowly to the fence and stop. Two men climbed out of the truck and ran into the car. The car sped off. Why had the men abandoned their truck? Something was wrong.

Guerreo sounded an alarm and rushed down off the roof. Room by room, he told everyone he saw to leave the building. He didn't know it, but he had only three minutes to complete his task. He had warned two floors when a loud explosion blasted through the entire military base. The blast was so violent it tore off the front side of the building. "There was a loud bang, everything

Saudi Arabia is a country composed of several smaller states, covering about 900,000 square miles (1,448,410 square kilometers). The city of Riyadh is its capital, and the city of Mecca is considered sacred to those who practice Islam. As much of the country is too harsh for agriculture, most of the Saudi population now lives in cities.

went dark," Guerreo told a CNN reporter. "There was dust and debris flying around everywhere. I was just spun around . . . Somebody near me was knocked down to the ground and unconscious."

The Attack on U.S. Servicemen in Saudi Arabia on June 25, 1996

In the end, the powerful explosion toppled the apartment tower where U.S. troops lived alongside French, British, and Saudi military personnel. Nineteen Americans were killed, and hundreds of others were injured, including men and women from Saudi Arabia, India, Egypt, Jordan, Indonesia, and the Philippines. It was the second time that year that the U.S. military had been targeted in Saudi Arabia.

Seven months earlier, in November 1995, a car bomb exploded outside a U.S. training facility in Riyadh, Saudi Arabia. The bomb tore through the building filled with U.S. and Saudi military personnel. The wreckage of the mangled building went up in flames. Six people were killed, including five Americans.

The attacks raised many questions. Who had carried them out? Could the facilities have been better protected? Who were the intended targets?

It was presumed that both attacks were part of a wave of anti-American terrorism directed by militant Islamic forces. Many Muslim communities feel that they are under attack, both literally and symbolically. Many resent the foreign presence in and occupation of traditionally Muslim lands, particularly Saudi Arabia, Lebanon, Chechnya, and Israel. They feel that American culture is taking over the world at the expense of traditional Islamic values. Some of the more extreme Islamic groups believe that the United States and Israel have conspired to rid the world of Islam entirely.

Terrorism is a form of political violence used to assert the demands of groups that aren't allied with a particular nation or government. Terrorist acts such as car bombings, hijackings, and the taking of hostages allow groups to intimidate and threaten a large number of people using relatively few resources.

Terrorist organizations usually operate in secret. To protect their identities, they often rely on a number of cells, or small units, to complete a mission. For example, one cell might be responsible for financing an attack, one for planning, one for supplying weapons, and one for carrying out the attack. This ensures that if one person is caught he can only expose his own cell, since he has no information about the rest of the organization.

Without knowing who is responsible for what, it is difficult to predict when a terrorist attack could occur or to retaliate against it. In 1995 and 1996, the U.S. military, one of the most powerful military forces in the world, fell victim to devastating attacks at the hands of a few men, a few civilian vehicles, and a few thousand pounds of explosive material.

The Grand Mosque in Mecca, Islam's holiest shrine, is visited by tens of thousands of pilgrims every year as part of the traditional hajj pilgrimage.

SAUDI ARABIA: A LAND OF TRADITION IN CHANGING TIMES

CHAPTER

1

For almost 4,000 years, the way of life in the region now known as Saudi Arabia changed very little. Located in the Middle East on the Arabian Peninsula, the area saw few ancient peoples settle permanently on its harsh desert lands. Instead, nomadic tribes crossed the peninsula in order to trade with lands across the desert. In time, traders began to settle in the more livable parts of the peninsula near the Persian Gulf, the Red Sea, and in the plateaus in the middle of the peninsula, where oases made some farming possible.

Because the land had few resources, most of the nomads and farmers who lived there were poor. The land had few urban centers, even though it was home to Islam's two most sacred shrines, Mecca and Medina. Even the influx of visitors making pilgrimages to these destinations could not improve the region's overall welfare. Then, in the twentieth century, Saudi Arabia changed dramatically with the discovery of a single resource: oil.

Geography and Natural Resources

Saudi Arabia covers about three-fourths of the Arabian Peninsula. To the west, the country is bordered by the Red Sea; to the north, by Jordan, Iraq, and Kuwait; to the east, the Persian Gulf; and to the south, by the United Arab Emirates, Oman, and Yemen.

The landscape is virtually barren. Western Saudi Arabia is covered with rugged mountains and ocean plains. Vast deserts spread over areas to the north, south, and east. The middle region is a high plateau.

The world's largest known oil reserves—about one-quarter of the world's total—are located beneath the Persian Gulf off the eastern coast of Saudi Arabia and in its eastern deserts. Because Saudi Arabia has a relatively small demand for oil, the country sells most of its oil overseas, making it a leader in the international crude oil market.

History

The first inhabitants of Arabia were most likely nomads from the north regions now known as Jordan and Iraq. These nomads sailed across the Red Sea to trade with the great river valley civilization of the Nile (now Egypt) and crossed the

In this 1948 photo, a workman covers oil processing equipment in Dhahran with reflective aluminum paint to keep it from overheating.

deserts to trade with the Tigris-Euphrates (present-day Iraq), another great civilization.

Living conditions improved in 1000 BC, when the camel saddle was invented. This allowed camels—the only animal able to cross the great expanses of desert—to be used to transport goods and people reliably. The silks, spices, gold, textiles, and other goods that were traded brought wealth to parts of the region. Arabia's first settlements, many of which started as stops for camel caravans crossing the desert, developed along the southwestern coast, where the climate and topography were less severe.

King Ibn Saud of Saudi Arabia, in a 1943 photo. Saudi Arabia has been an absolute, hereditary monarchy since Ibn Saud claimed the throne in 1932.

Before the development of Saudi Arabia's oil industry in the mid-1900s, most people lived in rural areas and made their livings as farmers, herders, and traders. Oil was discovered before World War I (1914–1918). However, it wasn't until the 1930s, when America was given permission to develop the oil, that Saudi Arabia was able to profit from the resource.

With the money made from the oil industry, King Ibn Saud worked to modernize his country. He strengthened Saudi Arabia's water supply, agriculture, manufacturing, and public health. As Saudi Arabia's oil industry developed into one of the world's largest, people migrated to the cities for work. Currently, approximately three-quarters of Saudi Arabia's population of 21 million people live and work in large cities like Riyadh, Jeddah, Dhahran, and Mecca.

Today, Saudi Arabia is the world's largest exporter of petroleum and a leading producer of natural gas.

However, because Saudi Arabia is such a traditional and deeply religious society—all Saudi citizens are Muslims—the influx of wealth, technology, non-Muslims, and Western ideas and practices has created many conflicts over the years. Also, the wealth in Saudi Arabia is far from evenly distributed. The average annual income in U.S. dollars is $8,060. The disparity of wealth is also responsible for internal conflict.

Government

Saudi Arabia is an absolute monarchy ruled by the Al Saud family. The current monarchy dates back to 1932, when Ibn Saud reclaimed tribal lands lost by his father, named these lands Saudi Arabia, and made himself king. Ibn Saud was survived by thirty sons, four of whom went on to become king.

The king holds executive and legislative powers. As Custodian of the Two Holy Mosques, the king is also responsible for protecting Islam's most holy shrines—Mecca and Medina. Saudi Arabia has no written constitution, but in 1992 a law declared that the constitution of Saudi Arabia was the Koran, the Muslim holy book, and the sunna, a collection of the sayings and practices of the prophet Muhammad, the founder of Islam. The king must seek approval for many decisions from the ulema, a group of the country's religious leaders.

The Qaaba, a black stone cube in the center of Mecca's Grand Mosque, is circled by thousands of Muslims as part of the ceremony marking the end of their annual pilgrimage.

Religion

Before the birth of Islam in seventh century AD, Arabia was home to a variety of religions. Many of these were pagan (believing in many gods or no god) and polytheistic (believing in more than one god), such as the worship of the Sun and the Moon and the sacrifice of animals to appease and give thanks to the gods. Traders introduced religions from other regions, such as Judaism and Christianity. But the religion that took hold on the region was Islam, preached by the prophet Muhammad.

Muhammad was born around 570 AD into a prosperous trading family in the city of Mecca. When Muhammad's father died, his uncle sent him to live in the desert with bedouin tribes in order to learn traditional Arabian values, such as humility and hospitality. When he returned, he worked in his family's trading business. During his business trips, he visited several Christian and Jewish communities. Their belief in one god and reliance on scriptures influenced Muhammad deeply. He created his own religion, Islam. He believed himself to be the final messenger of God, following the Biblical prophets Abraham, Moses, David, and Jesus.

Islam, which means "surrender" or "submission" in Arabic, teaches that there is only one god, Allah. According to Islamic belief, Muhammad was alone in the mountains near Mecca when the angel Gabriel appeared to him. Gabriel revealed a holy message from God and commanded

SAUDI ARABIA'S RELIGIOUS POLICE

In addition to a regular police force, Saudi Arabia maintains a religious police force. Called the Mutawaa'in, the group enforces religious and moral codes. Known for their brutality and fanaticism, the Mutawaa'in can beat or arrest people for the slightest infraction of Islamic law, including improper dress, the consumption of alcohol, gambling, or the neglect of prayer and fasting requirements.

They can break up public gatherings of women and arrest unrelated men and women if they are found together. Women who do not wear an *abaya*, a black garment that covers the entire body, and who fail to cover their face and hair are subject to physical and verbal harassment.

Muhammad to deliver this message to the people. The Koran, which means "the recitation" in Arabic, is Muhammad's transcript of Gabriel's message.

Society

Although the development of the oil industry led to the spread of modern conveniences, Saudi Arabian society remains extremely traditional and conservative. Cultural and political life is determined largely by Islamic values. To be considered a citizen, a Saudi must be Muslim. The majority of Saudis belong to the Sunni branch of Islam. Sunni Muslims, sometimes called fundamentalists by Westerners, practice a strict interpretation of Islam.

Since the kingdom was founded, the government has maintained strict control over every aspect of society. Newspapers, magazines, and television stations that criticize the royal family can be banned or shut down entirely if the government so chooses.

Saudi Arabia has a rich history of folk dance and music, but public displays of music and dance are forbidden, excepting all-male performances of traditional religious or tribal works. Saudi citizens are free to listen to the radio and television, but only in the privacy of their own homes. Sports is one of the few aspects of Saudi culture that is not directly influenced by religion. Soccer, volleyball, basketball, and golf are among the most popular.

Women in Saudi Arabia

On the whole, the Islamic world views women very differently than does the Western world. In Saudi Arabia, women, including foreigners, have few political or social rights. They are not allowed to drive. They are forbidden to travel without a male relative or his written permission.

In this 1990 photo, two Saudi women wear abayas with veils that cover their faces, called burkas. The two younger girls wear only the abayas.

They are not allowed to go to many public places, such as stores, when men are present. They must board city buses by separate rear entrances and sit in specially designated sections. They cannot seek medical treatment without the consent of a male relative. In addition, a woman cannot appear in public without wearing an abaya, a black garment that covers her entire body. She must also cover her head and face.

Women have access to free but segregated education through the university level. According to the U.S. State Department, women make up more than 58 percent of all university students. However, women are not allowed to study certain subjects, including engineering, journalism, and architecture. Men may study overseas; women may do so only if accompanied by a male from their immediate family.

Most employment opportunities for women are in education and health care, although a few work in business, philanthropy, banking, retail sales, and the media. Most work-places are segregated by gender. The U.S. State Department estimates that women make up 5 percent of the formal work force and own 20 percent of the businesses, although a male relative must represent them in financial transactions.

In 1984, this polyethylene plant was built in Al-Jubail, Saudi Arabia, as part of a joint venture between Saudi Arabia's Al-Jubail Petrochemical Company and the Exxon Corporation.

RELATIONS BETWEEN THE UNITED STATES AND SAUDI ARABIA

CHAPTER

For more than sixty years, the United States has maintained friendly, if occasionally strained, relations with Saudi Arabia. The two countries share concerns over regional security and development.

Diplomatic relations between the two countries were established in 1933, the same year that King Ibn Saud granted Standard Oil, an American company, the right to explore and drill for oil in Saudi Arabia. The United States opened an embassy in Jeddah in 1944. In 1984 the embassy moved to Riyadh, Saudi Arabia's capital. In addition to the embassy, the United States maintains consulates in Jeddah and Dhahran.

Saudi Arabia remained neutral for most of World War II (1939–1945). However, it was sympathetic to the Allied cause and allowed the United States to build an airfield in Dhahran. In 1945, Saudi Arabia joined the United Nations and the Arab League. Saudi Arabia was sympathetic to Arab countries, but its foreign policy toward Western nations, particularly the United States, tended to be more moderate than most other Middle Eastern countries.

In 1951, Saudi Arabia agreed to let the United States use the air base for another five years in exchange for technical aid and permission to purchase weaponry. Between World War II and 1975, the United States provided $328.4 million in economic and military aid to Saudi Arabia.

The alliance between the United States and Saudi Arabia ensures that the United States, one of the world's biggest consumers of Saudi oil, has a moderate ally and reliable energy source in the oil-rich Middle East. In turn, Saudi Arabia can depend on the United States for technological assistance and military defense.

The Persian Gulf War

With one-tenth of the globe's oil supply, the Middle Eastern country of Kuwait was one of the world's wealthiest countries. Its northern neighbor, Iraq, was also oil rich. But under the

Hundreds of Kuwaiti oil fields were set afire by Iraqi troops fleeing American forces during the 1991 Gulf War. U.S. forces helped the Kuwaitis put out the fires, but the environmental effects of the smoke affected air quality for thousands of miles.

leadership of Saddam Hussein, Iraq's military spending pushed the country to the brink of bankruptcy. Hussein blamed Iraq's debt on Kuwait. He accused Kuwait of a U.S.-backed conspiracy to flood the world market with cheap oil in order to keep oil prices low. Hussein demanded that Kuwait raise its oil prices. When Kuwait refused, Hussein issued an ultimatum: pay $10 billion in damages or face invasion. Hussein backed this threat by sending Iraqi troops to the Iraq-Kuwait border.

Many countries were concerned by Hussein's actions. If Hussein successfully invaded Kuwait, it would mean that Iraq would control one-fifth of the world's oil supply. Hussein told U.S. representatives in confidence that he was merely try-ing to intimidate Kuwait and would not carry out an invasion. However, in August 1990, Iraqi troops rolled across the border and invaded Kuwait.

The United States organized an international coali-tion to help Kuwait regain its independence. The coalition included Egypt, Saudi Arabia, Syria, France, Great Britain, and the Soviet Union. In order to carry out any military action, the coalition would need a Middle Eastern base. The United States turned to its longtime ally Saudi Arabia. The United States warned the country, which did not have a strong military force, that they could be the next Iraqi target. Saudi Arabia agreed to let coalition troops into the country. Almost immediately, more than 250,000 U.S. troops moved into Saudi Arabia. It was the largest military deployment of U.S. troops since the Vietnam War (1955–1975). In January 1991, coalition forces moved into Kuwait and quickly forced Iraqi troops to withdraw. As the Iraqi troops retreated back into Iraq, they set fire to oil wells across Kuwait and blew up oil pipelines and tankers. It is estimated that 8 million barrels of oil were spilled into the Persian Gulf. The oil fires and spills created an enormous ecological disaster.

Call for a War on America

After the war, Saudi Arabia vowed to improve its military. In order to build its armed forces, it cut back its spending on

CULTURE CLASH—REAL OR SYMBOLIC?

Many journalists and Middle East experts thought that Saudi Arabian society would be affected by the arrival of thousands of American and foreign troops and media crews during the Persian Gulf War. Some worried that the Westerners' comparatively liberal and non-Islamic attitudes about everything from sex to alcohol to the role of women in society would corrupt the desert kingdom. A few hoped that the foreigners would prompt reforms such as more visibility and political rights for women.

In the end, Saudi society seemed unaffected. An official with the Riyadh Chamber of Commerce told the *Los Angeles Times*, "It was a totally false premise, the idea that the pressure of 400,000 Americans in Saudi Arabia would inevitably change us. It is not that we don't change. We change every day. But it was a false premise that we were an isolated island out of touch with the world."

Aside from the influx during the Gulf War, tens of thousands of foreigners work in Saudi Arabia. But foreign troops and civilians are isolated from Saudi society, largely confined to compounds and isolated along the Red Sea coast and the oil producing areas of Dhahran. For decades, Saudi Arabia had been exposed to Western culture through travel, media, movies, music, and the Internet. Despite these influences, Saudi society remains traditional and conservative.

social programs at home and financial aid to other Arab countries. It spent billions of dollars on U.S. planes, tanks, missiles, and other military equipment. Hundreds of American military personnel stayed in Saudi Arabia to protect its airspace and to help train its military. The United States

During the Gulf War, thousands of Iraqi soldiers surrendered to U.S. forces. This group of captives was marched through the Kuwait desert on February 24, 1991, accompanied by U.S. Marine Second Division vehicles.

was also allowed to keep its own military supplies in the country in case U.S. forces were again called in to defend Saudi Arabia.

Together, these actions upset many Muslims in Saudi Arabia and abroad. They worried that Saudi Arabia had become a puppet for U.S. policy. They also felt that the continued U.S. military presence was an affront to Islam. Opposed to the establishment of Israel in what was once mostly Arab territories, many Arabs deeply resented the United States's ongoing support of Israel. To have an Arab country like Saudi Arabia host U.S. forces was deemed a betrayal by many Arabs.

In August 1995, Osama bin Laden, a wealthy Saudi exile who was organizing a worldwide militia of Islamic fundamentalists, wrote an open letter to King Fahd of Saudi Arabia. He argued that Islam was under attack by U.S. foreign policy and by the spread of American culture, which seems decadent and corrupt to many Muslims. He called for a campaign of guerrilla attacks to drive U.S. forces out of the holy kingdom.

In 1996, bin Laden issued a fatwa, or religious decree, calling for all Muslims to declare war on America. Bin Laden found Muslim sympathizers all over the world, including in Saudi Arabia. Many Saudis agreed with bin Laden that their country had been corrupted by wealth and Western influence. They were angered that certain elements of Saudi Arabian society, including Saudi Arabia's royal family, did not adhere to strict Islamic tenets. They condemned wealthy Arab sheiks who drank, indulged in promiscuous sex, and spent extravagant sums on personal comfort. They were angered by Saudi Arabia's alliance with Western, non-Islamic countries, particularly the United States.

Anti-American sentiment was on the rise.

The city of Riyadh has overrun the mud and brick walls that once protected it from invaders, becoming a large and wealthy modern city undergoing constant renovation. It has been Saudi Arabia's capital since 1932.

THE RIYADH BOMBING

Situated in the middle of Saudi Arabia, Riyadh, the country's capital, is one of the most religiously conservative cities in Saudi Arabia. However, the city also boasts modern buildings, office towers, shopping malls, and American fast-food outlets. By midmorning, Riyadh's streets are usually crowded with cars and delivery trucks.

In the heart of Riyadh, near a busy shopping center, is the headquarters for the Saudi Arabian National Guard. A U.S. Army program that provided military and civilian advisers to the National Guard had offices in the three-story building. For the roughly 200 people working inside the building on the morning of November 13, 1995, the day began uneventfully. At 11:30 AM, U.S. Army major James Johnson was sitting in his office, located on the top floor. Johnson, a scholar on the Middle East and a communications specialist, worked with the Saudi National Guard. A few minutes later, he stood up to leave for a training exercise. In an instant, he was thrown to the floor when a massive explosion rocked the building. The blast seemed to come from nowhere.

When Johnson looked up, the entire front of the building was gone. He was staring at open sky and piles of burning rubble. He and fellow soldier David Dewitt crawled out from the ruins and tried to assist other victims of the bombing.

When the blast occurred, William Mooney was working in his office. Suddenly, he found himself covered in blood. He suffered serious cuts and bruises, but luckily, his office chair shielded him from more serious injuries. The man with whom he shared his office was not so lucky; he died in the blast.

The powerful blast was heard by diplomats in embassies miles away. Store and office windows throughout the neighborhood were shattered. The explosion set fire to the building. The flames burned briefly, sending up black clouds of smoke that could be seen around the city. Cars parked in the streets near the building were reduced to charred, twisted piles of metal, their windows blown out by the force of the blast.

Security personnel scour the parking lot of the Saudi Arabian National Guard headquarters, searching for evidence among the debris following the detonation of a car bomb on November 13, 1995.

The bombing, which occurred near the ground-floor snack bar, appeared to have been timed to go off when many U.S. employees would be eating lunch and most Saudis would be at prayer. When the bomb exploded, most of those who died and suffered serious injuries were in the lunchroom.

Three days after the attack, Major Johnson was lying in a military hospital bed. His neck and face were covered with wounds and stitches. His right arm was shattered, and his back was cut by shards of glass. "I feel sorry for Saudi Arabia," he told the *Boston Globe*. "It looks like this epidemic of terrorism is coming here now, in what I thought was the safest country in the world."

Because Saudi Arabian police were not accustomed to sharing information, gathering clues was difficult for U.S. investigators. Compounding the problem, the crime scene in Riyadh had not been carefully isolated from outside interference.

In the final tally, seven people were killed in the blast, including five from the United States. Sixty others were injured, including thirty-seven U.S. citizens.

Looking for Answers

Although it wasn't clear who had carried out the bombings, there was no shortage of suspects. Several underground groups had openly threatened to attack Saudi leadership and Western forces. Just hours after the explosion, three militant Islamic groups—the "Tigers of the Gulf," the "Movement for Islamic Change," and the "Combatant Partisans of God"—claimed responsibility for the bombing.

The bombing was the first terrorist attack against the American military in Saudi Arabia. "We're not used to it," a Saudi official told the *Washington Post.* "This is a shocking experience for everyone here."

Saudi Arabia's King Fahd quickly condemned the attacks, calling the bombing a criminal act that was foreign to Saudi Arabia's society, beliefs, and

The men who confessed to the Riyadh bombing were publicly beheaded by Saudi police. Beheadings and amputations are a common part of the Saudi Arabian justice system.

religion. Prince Bandar bin Sultan, the Saudi ambassador to the United States, also denounced the attack as a despicable act.

U.S. president Bill Clinton pledged to bring those responsible to justice. The U.S. Embassy offered a $2 million reward for information about those behind the bombing, in addition to an $800,000 reward offered by the Saudi government. More than a dozen Federal Bureau of Investigation (FBI) agents and evidence specialists were sent to Saudi Arabia to help with the investigation. Together, U.S. investigators and Saudi security searched through rubble looking for clues.

The FBI had difficulty carrying out its investigation. The crime scene had not been carefully isolated, and investigators were frustrated in their inability to find critical evidence. They also had some communication problems with Saudi investigators. Despite these difficulties, on April 22, 1996, the minister of the interior of Saudi Arabia, Prince Nayef, announced the arrest of four young men in connection with the Riyadh bombing. Shortly afterward, the four Saudis appeared on national television and gave almost identical confessions.

The men said that they had been influenced by Islamic terrorists outside Saudi Arabia. They claimed that they had never met Osama bin Laden, but that he was their inspiration. In a confession reported by the *New York Times*, twenty-eight-year-old Muslih al-Shamrani admitted: "I did travel to Afghanistan. I was trained in the use of light and heavy weapons. In Afghanistan, I met people of various nationalities who charged rulers and scholars with blasphemy. We decided to carry out an act of jihad inside Saudi Arabia." He returned to Saudi Arabia and joined with three friends. The men plotted an attack against the Saudi government and its U.S. military support. They said that they had targeted the training center because of the easy access to the street in front of the building. They confessed to smuggling explosives, rifles, and ammunition into the country from Yemen.

Prince Nayef said that the men would be tried and punished according to Islamic law. The usual penalty for murder is public beheading by sword. On May 31, the men were executed in a public square in Riyadh. The United States was pleased that the men had been brought to justice, but it was upset that justice had been carried out without their consultation. FBI investigators had hoped to interview the suspects. They never got the chance. The rapid execution cut short a U.S. investigation as to whether the men had acted alone, as they said, or with the direct support of another country or a larger terrorist network.

After the executions, underground extremists threatened to retaliate. They promised more attacks against U.S. troops in Saudi Arabia.

The truck bomb that exploded near Khobar Towers, seen here, killed nineteen U.S. citizens and injured more than 300 others. The truck was carrying 2.5 tons (2,250 kilograms) of explosives.

KHOBAR TOWERS

About 2,500 U.S. service-people were based at Khobar Towers, a large complex of apartment, administrative, and recreational buildings close to the King Abdul-Aziz Naval Air Base in Al-Khobar. The buildings sprawled across a dozen acres. Khobar Towers's residents included American, British, and French troops. Many of the men and women were air force personnel. Their main mission was to enforce a ban on flights by Iraqi military aircraft that had been put into effect after the Persian Gulf War.

Following the Riyadh bombing, U.S. authorities surrounded the

Khobar Towers complex with a chain-link fence and waist-high concrete barriers. They increased patrols by security police and stationed guards on the roof to watch for suspicious behavior.

On the night of June 25, 1996, a tanker truck and a white Chevrolet Caprice pulled into the Khobar housing complex. They parked next to a fence in a public parking lot near the edge of the compound. It was 10 PM. Most of the military personnel were getting ready for bed. An American guard standing sentry spotted the suspicious vehicles and warned Saudi patrol guards. The American went to evacuate the building while the Saudi guards went to question the men in the truck. When the men saw the Saudi guards approaching, they quickly climbed into the Chevrolet and sped off. The guards went to help warn compound residents, but they were too late.

Moments later, the truck, stuffed with 5,000 pounds of explosives, blew up. The powerful explosion left a crater thirty-five feet deep and eighty-five feet long. It completely sheared off the face of the apartment complex. Windows shattered throughout the compound. The blast was heard as far as twenty miles away. Nineteen U.S. servicemen were killed and more than 500 others were injured, including Americans, Saudis, and Indians.

U.S. Air Force staff sergeant Tyler Christie told the Associated Press: "I heard a deafening noise and then the windows were shattered and the walls fell in. People were running everywhere. A few buildings were destroyed." A young Saudi who was near the scene told the *New York Times*: "We thought it was the end of the world. Some were crying; some just sat on the ground and held their ears."

When the explosion occurred, Ruth Rosser was making dessert for her husband, Tom. The couple lived in a foreigners' compound about half a mile from the explosion. "There was a big boom, a tremendous, indescribable sound, and glass was coming down like rain—we could hear it coming down," she told

Saudi Arabians examine the 85-foot (26-meter) crater left by the Khobar Towers explosion.

the *New York Times*. "It's amazing no one here was hurt. But it makes me much more unsettled. The American Consulate puts out warnings, but you think it won't happen here, it won't happen to me."

Immediately following the bombing, U.S. secretary of state Warren Christopher interrupted a tour of the Middle East and flew to Dhahran. His first stop was at the hospital where many of the injured were recovering. He wanted to talk to the victims firsthand, to see what they had experienced and to offer his sympathy. Many of the soldiers were covered with bruises, bandages, and stitches. One soldier said he had been watching the evening news when he looked out the window

Prince Al-Saud *(left)* looks on as U.S. secretary of state Warren Christopher is interviewed by the press outside of the Khobar Towers. The U.S. military personnel who lived in the towers were relocated.

and saw a fireball coming from out of nowhere. The fireball came through the window and knocked him over. Another soldier told Christopher that he was talking on the telephone with his back to the wall; suddenly, the wall wasn't there. Everything went dark and the soldier went flying. Others compared the experience to a huge earthquake.

After talking with the soldiers, Christopher toured the bomb site. The eight-story concrete building was missing its entire outer wall. Mattresses, pipes, and wires hung from the exposed floors. Many other buildings in the area were also damaged. Surveying the site, Christopher said it was a miracle that more people weren't killed. He promised to find the terrorists and bring them to justice, no matter how long it took.

Security Questions

After the Khobar Towers bombing—the second attack against U.S. military forces in Saudi Arabia that year— military officials were forced to explain why the base was not better protected. In the weeks leading up to the bomb-ings, the United States had received several threats against Americans and U.S. military installa-tions in Saudi Arabia. Many of these came just before and after the execution of the four Saudis who confessed to the bombing in Riyadh.

U.S. military officials were criticized

Should U.S. Forces Be in Saudi Arabia?

Franklin D. Roosevelt recognized our security interests in the [Middle East] region, particularly in Saudi Arabia, almost 60 years ago. First, the health of our economy is directly linked to the gulf, which holds two-thirds of the world's proven oil reserves. Second, stability in the region is critical for long-term prospects for Arab-Israeli peace. Third, the region has key navigation choke points along air and sea lanes that connect Europe and the Mediterranean with Africa, Asia and the Indian Ocean. Those routes are critical to our ability to send and receive products from those areas . . .

The terrorist bombing that killed 19 brave young Americans is a national tragedy . . . But we should not compound that tragedy by losing sight of why they were there. They were defending the vital national interests of the United States of America. We must continue to defend those interests in Saudi Arabia as long as they exist. Neither terrorists nor a retreat-in-the-face-of-danger mentality should ever be allowed to drive our national policy.

—H. Norman Schwarzkopf, retired U.S. Army general *USA Today*, July 31, 1996

Members of the 33rd Fighter Wing bow their heads during the memorial service held to commemorate the lives of those killed at the Khobar Towers.

for not taking proper precautions. The building that was hit hardest by the bomb was separated from a public road and an amusement park parking lot by only thirty-five yards and a low concrete barrier. "This building we were in, we constantly joked that we were a fine target, out in this corner, right next to the park," Staff Sergeant Anthony Overbay told the *Atlanta Journal-Constitution*.

Investigations were conducted by several congressional committees and a U.S. Defense Department task force headed by retired U.S. Army general Wayne Downing. The investigations centered on whether the U.S. military had been given adequate information about threats and whether the military had taken proper security measures.

The Downing report found that the U.S. military failed to respond to repeated warnings of a possible terrorist attack. For example, the Dhahran air base had no high-tech sensors or security cameras. Instead, air force security guards kept watch over the base, standing in the 120-degree heat, equipped with only binoculars. The report said that the fence around Khobar Towers should have been extended to distance the apartment complex from a possible blast. Defense Secretary William Perry accepted the recommendations and requested that millions of dollars be spent on improving security at U.S. military bases abroad.

Relocation

After the Khobar Towers bombing, the U.S. Defense Department and the Saudi government agreed to split the estimated $200 million cost of moving 4,200 U.S. military personnel to other bases to protect them from further terrorist attacks.

U.S. soldiers from the Al-Khobar base were moved to the more isolated Prince Sultan air base about sixty miles south of Riyadh. Many U.S. military personnel stationed in Riyadh were also relocated to bases outside the city. Both locations tightened their security. The Prince Sultan air base featured a swimming pool, shopping mall, and a Baskin-Robbins ice cream parlor. It also boasted wire, dirt, and concrete barriers and ten guard towers. One resident, Lt. Col. Joseph Worrell, told a *New York Times* reporter, "It sort of gives you the impression of a prison."

Officials from the Federal Bureau of Investigation pick through debris that has been identified as remains from the truck bomb that destroyed the Khobar Towers.

INVESTIGATION INTO THE KHOBAR TOWERS BOMBING

T he day after the Khobar Towers bombing, a team of forty FBI agents flew to Saudi Arabia to assist Saudi authorities in a joint investigation of the attack. The United States offered a $2 million reward for information leading to the perpetrators, in addition to a $3 million reward offered by the Saudi government. U.S. officials praised Saudi Arabia for its promise of support and cooperation in finding those responsible and bringing them to justice.

Investigators felt certain that the attack had been carried out by a well-connected group of Islamic extremists. They were less certain about which group was responsible. The bombing seemed to be the work of professionals. The carefully chosen target, the planned escape, and the use of large quantities of military-grade explosives and sophisticated fuses led investigators to believe that the attack had been organized in advance and the bombers carefully trained. One group that stood out as a possible suspect was Hezbollah, an Islamic terrorist group that receives support from Iran. If the terrorists had been supported by a foreign country, Iran was one of the main suspects. The country had a history of hostility toward Saudi Arabia and the United States, and it had been accused of sponsoring terrorists in the past. In addition, some Saudi investigators thought that the explosives had been smuggled into the country from Lebanon, where Hezbollah is most active.

However, as the Riyadh bombing proved, Saudi Arabia had a growing number of its own militant Islamic extremists who opposed the Saudi and U.S. governments. Indeed, exiled Saudi Osama bin Laden had called on Muslims worldwide to attack Americans, particularly U.S. military forces. The list of possible suspects was large.

A Stalled Investigation

During the next year, the investigation into the Khobar Towers bombing seemed to unravel. Many theories surfaced but there was little concrete evidence. Some blamed the breakdown of the investigation on the uneasy relationship between U.S. and Saudi investigators. Saudi Arabia's police were not used to letting foreigners help with their investigations. The FBI wasn't accustomed to seeking permission to collect and examine evidence.

Top U.S. officials publicly criticized Saudi Arabia's investigation efforts. U.S. attorney general Janet Reno and FBI director Louis Freeh charged that Saudi Arabia was conducting its investigation in secret, even though it had promised to cooperate with U.S. investigators. They complained that U.S. officials were given only summaries of the investigation, and they accused Saudi Arabia of not sharing important information. It was unusual for the United States to criticize its ally Saudi Arabia so openly.

A year and a half after the bombing, U.S. officials had the unpleasant task of telling the victims' families that they still did not know who carried out the attack. In December 1997, Reno, Freeh, and other officials met privately with the victims' families at a day-long counseling session and dinner. They promised to press on with the investigation. "There was great respect for us, but little information," one mother told the *New York Times*. "They don't have anything concrete."

U.S. officials acknowledged that they had reached no conclusions about who was responsible. They feared they would never get the Saudi cooperation necessary to complete the investigation. "By ourselves, there's not much we can do," a U.S. official told a CNN reporter. Even though

Attorney General Janet Reno consults with FBI director Louis Freeh at a Senate Appropriations Subcommittee hearing on terrorism, which was formed out of concern for the growing number of terror attacks against the United States.

Freeh had traveled to Saudi Arabia twice to make personal appeals to King Fahd and other top Saudi officials, FBI agents were not allowed to interrogate suspects or access the Saudis' information. "It's their country, after all," the official said. "FBI jurisdiction overseas is limited by the invitation of the host country."

Almost two years after the investigation started, the FBI pulled its investigators out of Saudi Arabia, leaving behind only one agent. Although it seemed that the U.S. investigation was over, the Departments of Justice and Defense vowed that they would not close the investigation.

U.S. Indictments, Saudi Justice

In June 2001, a U.S. grand jury indicted thirteen Saudis and one Lebanese national for the Khobar Towers bombing. Nine of the fourteen men were charged with forty-six separate felony counts, including murder, use of a weapon of mass destruction, and conspiracy to kill Americans. The men were said to be members of an organization called Saudi Hezbollah, a Saudi Shiite group with alleged ties to Iranian-backed Hezbollah. Some were already being held in Saudi jails. The others were at large. The United States does not have an extradition treaty with Saudi Arabia, and Saudi Arabia was not interested in extraditing the suspects. Saudi Arabian officials said that their own courts would handle the case. It seemed unlikely that any of the men would be brought to the United States to stand trial.

A year later, on June 1, 2002, Saudi Arabia sentenced some of the men in connection with the bombing. Prince Ahmed Ibn Abdul Aziz, the brother of King Fahd and Saudi Arabia's deputy minister, did not specify how many people were sentenced or say what sentences would be imposed. He said that the bombing suspects had been sentenced under Islamic law and that the sentences still had to be approved by the supreme justice council and the king. According to the *New York Times*, Prince Ahmed told a Saudi newspaper that the verdicts would be announced "at the right time." U.S. investigators were concerned that the men would be executed before they could question them, as happened in the case of the Riyadh bombing suspects.

New York City construction workers disassemble the wreckage of the World Trade Center's Building 7. The World Trade Center was attacked by terrorists on September 11, 2001.

GLOBAL TERRORISM: A NEW ERA IN FOREIGN RELATIONS

The attacks against the U.S. military installations in Saudi Arabia were part of a series of assaults carried out in the name of Islam. These include the 1997 shootings of international tourists in Luxor, Egypt; the 1998 bombing of the U.S. Embassies in Kenya and Tanzania; the 2000 bombing of the USS *Cole* off the coast of Yemen; and countless suicide bombings in Israel. The February 1993 bombing of the World Trade Center in New York City and the September 11, 2001, attacks on the World Trade Center and the Pentagon near Washington, D.C., demonstrated that Islamic terrorists were capable of striking Americans at home as well as abroad.

President George W. Bush has vowed to use any means necessary to track down and destroy foreign terror networks.

After the September 11 attacks, U.S. president George W. Bush announced a campaign against global terrorism. He asked the nations of the world to join the United States in its efforts, emphasizing the global nature of the problem. The campaign's first priority was to root out and destroy Saudi-born terrorist Osama bin Laden and his global terrorist network, Al Qaeda. But President Bush was clear: The campaign's long-term goal was to wipe out all terrorist groups.

The United States is in an awkward diplomatic position. It needs all the military and intelligence support it can get. What groups should be included on its list of terrorist organizations? For instance, should the United States include Hezbollah and Hamas, both anti-Israeli terrorist groups supported by Iran and Syria? Leaders from Egypt, Saudi Arabia, and Jordan indicated that Arab nations would not want to join a campaign that went beyond the destruction of Al Qaeda. Israeli leaders, however, expect the United States to include groups that have carried out so many terrorist acts against the Israelis.

The United States's campaign against bin Laden and Al Qaeda put a strain on its relationship with Saudi Arabia. Fifteen of the nineteen hijackers who carried out the September 11 attacks were from Saudi Arabia. It is suspected that Al Qaeda's terrorist camps were largely funded through Saudi Arabian charities.

As part of its campaign against terrorism, the United States asked many countries to freeze the assets of people and groups linked to bin Laden. But perhaps in an effort to ease diplomatic tension, it did not ask Saudi Arabia to do so. In a news conference held during a visit to Saudi Arabia in September 2001, according to the *New York Times*, Secretary of Defense Donald H. Rumsfeld remarked, "We understand that each country is different, each country lives in a different neighborhood, has a different perspective and has different sensitivities and different practices, and we do not expect every nation on earth to be publicly engaged in every single activity the United States is."

A New Generation of Holy Warriors

During the 1990s, thousands of Saudis left Saudi Arabia to wage an Islamic holy war. Many went to Afghanistan to train for jihad at Al Qaeda terrorist training camps. According to Saudi estimates quoted by the *New York Times*, as many as 25,000 Saudis received military training abroad since 1979.

Some U.S. officials are critical of the Saudi government for letting so many men leave to join military ventures abroad,

These Saudi Arabian men read an article about the capture of three Saudi Arabian suspects with ties to the Al Qaeda terror network. Because its members are in hiding all over the world, Al Qaeda terrorists are very difficult to locate.

despite the potential danger to the United States. Some point out that in the mid-1990s, when many terrorist attacks occurred, Saudi Arabia's economy was poor and unemployment was high. They charge that the Saudi government encouraged young men to leave Saudi Arabia rather than stay at home, where they might have caused political problems for Saudi Arabia.

Admittedly, the United States played a part in creating the new generation of Islamic terrorists. After the Soviet Union invaded Afghanistan in 1979, the United States and Saudi Arabia spent billions of dollars to train and equip

Muslim tribesmen to fight the Soviet-backed regime. Saudi Arabia, with U.S. approval, encouraged its young men to join the battle in the name of Islam. After Soviet troops withdrew in 1989, many of the Saudi men remained in Afghanistan. Eventually, many of these Saudis became more loyal to Islam than to their former backers in the United States and Saudi Arabia. Many eagerly joined bin Laden's call to jihad and recruited others to join them.

The Future of U.S.-Saudi Relations

The alliance between the United States and Saudi Arabia is complex; each has much to gain and much to lose. The United States remains dependent on Saudi Arabian oil; roughly one-fifth of its oil comes from Saudi Arabia. In the unstable Middle East, Saudi Arabia is one of the few countries with which the United States enjoys a stable relationship. But the stability is threatened by Saudi Arabia's radical Islamists.

The Saudi government is also threatened by radical Islamists, largely because of its alliance with the United States. Many radicals feel that the Al-Saud government is not legitimate because it has failed to protect Mecca and Medina from the presence of U.S. "infidels." Internal discontent with Saudi Arabia's government seems to be growing, along with the trend toward religious conservatism. In the past, Saudi Arabia has looked to the United States to defend it against potential enemies. Today, many Saudi citizens believe that the United States *is* the enemy. The more the Saudi Arabian government relies on the U.S. military, the more support it loses among its own people.

Meanwhile, terrorist threats continue. In May 2002, U.S. vice president Dick Cheney announced that new terrorist attacks against the United States—including attacks that could involve nuclear or biological weapons—were almost certain to occur. During a televised appearance on *FOX News Sunday,* Cheney said, "It could happen tomorrow, it could happen next week, it could happen next year, but they will keep trying. And we have to be prepared."

In this confusing and frightening diplomatic climate, the current strategy of the United States seems to be to promote understanding between the West and the Muslim world. In particular, the United States is looking to support more tolerant Islamic societies. In June 2002, U.S. deputy defense secretary Paul D. Wolfowitz told an Asian Security Conference, "These [tolerant] voices are essential to bridging the dangerous gap that now exists between the West and the Muslim world . . . . This larger war is a struggle against the enemies of tolerance and freedom, against the enemies of modernity and secularism, of pluralism and democracy, and real economic development."

Today, diplomats as well as average citizens are working to bring the United States and the Islamic world closer to a better understanding of each other. Their hope is for all to learn how to coexist more peacefully in the future.

GLOSSARY

Allies   In World War II, powers opposed to the Axis powers (Germany, Italy, and Japan), including Great Britain, the United States, France, and the Soviet Union.

Al Qaeda   A network of terrorist groups fronted by Islamic extremist and Saudi exile Osama bin Laden.

Arab League   Informal name for the Arab League of States, an association of independent Arab nations that promotes relations between members and coordinates policy on economic, cultural, and security matters.

consulate   The official residence of a government official who represents the interests of his or her country in a foreign nation.

extradite   To surrender a prisoner or fugitive to another country to stand trial for his or her crimes in that country.

fatwa   A religious decree issued by a religious leader; believers are obliged to comply.

guerrilla   A member of an independent military force that usually fights the main force of an occupied area by surprise raids and attacks.

Hamas   Arabic acronym for the Islamic Resistance Movement.

Hezbollah   In Arabic, "Party of God"; a Lebanon-based terrorist organization opposed to Israeli occupation of Lebanon and dedicated to the establishment of a Palestinian holy land.

indict   To make a formal accusation against someone.

infidel   A nonbeliever of a particular religion, particularly Christianity or Islam; one who has no religious beliefs.

Islam   A religion whose believers follow one god, Allah.

jihad   Arabic for "struggle"; used to describe a holy war, usually against enemies of Islam.

militant   An aggressive fighter.

monarchy   A state or government ruled by a monarch (someone who inherits rule over a state).

pilgrimage   A journey to a sacred place.

ulema   A group of religious authorities. In Saudi Arabia, the government must get the ulema's approval before making major political decisions.

FOR MORE INFORMATION

Americans for Middle East Understanding
475 Riverside Drive, Room 245
New York, NY 10115-0241
(212) 870-2053
Web site: http://www.ameu.org

Central Intelligence Agency (CIA)
Office of Public Affairs
Washington, DC 20505
(703) 482-0623
Web site: http://www.cia.gov

Federal Bureau of Investigation (FBI)
935 Pennsylvania Avenue NW, Room 7972
Washington, DC 20535
(202) 324-3000
Web site: http://www.fbi.gov

Foundation for Middle East Peace
1761 N Street NW
Washington, DC 20036
(202) 835-3650
Web site: http://www.fmep.org

Middle East Research and Information Project
1500 Massachusetts Avenue NW
Washington, DC 20005
(202) 223-3677
Web site: http://www.merip.org

U.S. Department of State
2201 C Street NW
Washington, DC 20520
(202) 647-4000
Web site: http://www.state.gov

Web Sites

Due to the changing nature of Internet links, the Rosen Publishing Group, Inc., has developed an online list of Web sites related to the subject of this book. This site is updated regularly. Please use this link to access the list:

http://www.rosenlinks.com/ta/auss/

FOR FURTHER READING

Fridell, Ron. *Terrorism: Political Violence at Home and Abroad*. Berkeley Heights, NJ: Enslow Publishers, Inc., 2001.

Goodwin, William. *Saudi Arabia*. San Diego, CA: Lucent Books, 2001.

Mulloy, Martin. *Saudi Arabia*. New York: Chelsea House, 1998.

Spencer, William. *Islamic Fundamentalism in the Modern World*. Brookfield, CT: Millbrook, 1995.

Williams, Mary E., ed. *The Middle East: Opposing Viewpoints*. San Diego, CA: Greenhaven Press, Inc., 2000.

BIBLIOGRAPHY

Atlanta Journal-Constitution, June 28, 1996: "Attack in Saudi Arabia: Responding to Terrorism."

Hart, Parker T. *Saudi Arabia and the United States: Birth of a Security Partnership.* Bloomington, IN: Indiana University Press, 1998.

New York Times. "Bombing in Saudi Arabia: The Saudis; West's Uneasy Presence: Infidels or Protectors?" June 28, 1996.

New York Times. "Bomb Kills 4 Americans in Saudi Arabia." November 14, 1995.

New York Times. "Four Confess on Saudi TV to Bombing of U.S. Center." April 23, 1996.

New York Times. "14 Indicted by U.S. in '96 Saudi Blast." June 22, 2001.

New York Times. "Saudi Militants Are Sentenced in '96 Bombing." June 2, 2002.

New York Times. "23 U.S. Troops Die in Truck Bombing." June 26, 1996.

Rubin, Barry. *Cauldron of Turmoil: America in the Middle East.* New York: Harcourt, Brace, Jovanovich, 1992.

USA Today. "Why Saudi Arabia Deserves Our Help." July 31, 1996.

INDEX

About the Author

Amanda Ferguson is a freelance writer living in Los Angeles.

Photo Credits

Cover © Reuters NewMedia Inc./Corbis; p. 5 © Maps.com/ Corbis; pp. 8–9, 11, 12, 16, 18, 20–21, 23, 26, 31, 32, 33, 36–37, 39, 40, 42, 44–45, 48, 50–51, 52, 54 © AP/Wide World Photos; p. 14 © AFP/Corbis; pp. 28–29 © Wolfgang Kaehler/Corbis.

Editor

Christine Poolos

Series Design and Layout

Geri Giordano